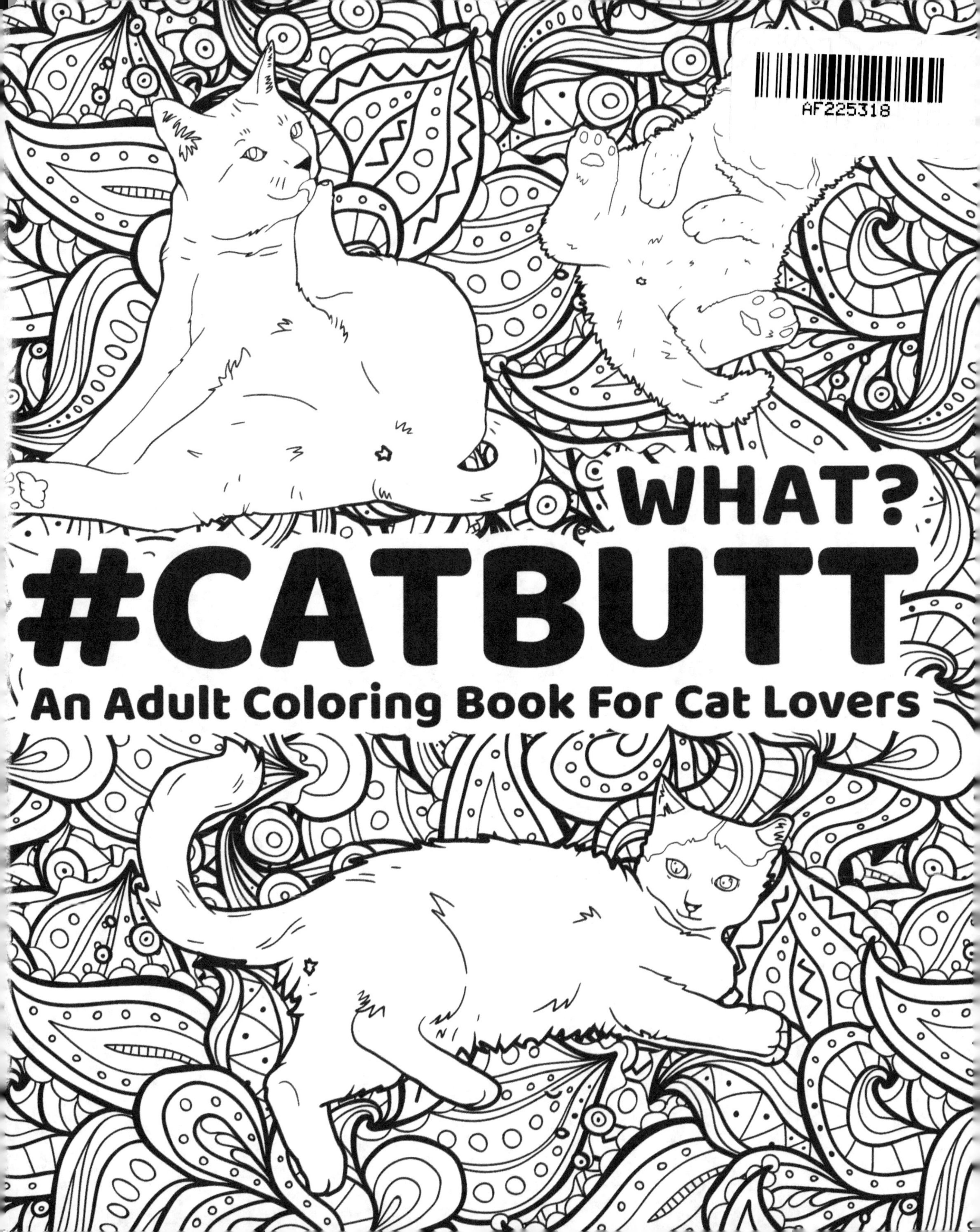

WHAT?
#CATBUTT
An Adult Coloring Book For Cat Lovers
AF225318

**Copyright © 2019
by Kolme Korkeudet Oy
All rights reserved**

No part of this book may be reproduced
in any form or by any electronic or
mechanical means, including information
storage and retrieval systems, without
written permission from the author,
except for the use of brief quotations
in a book review.

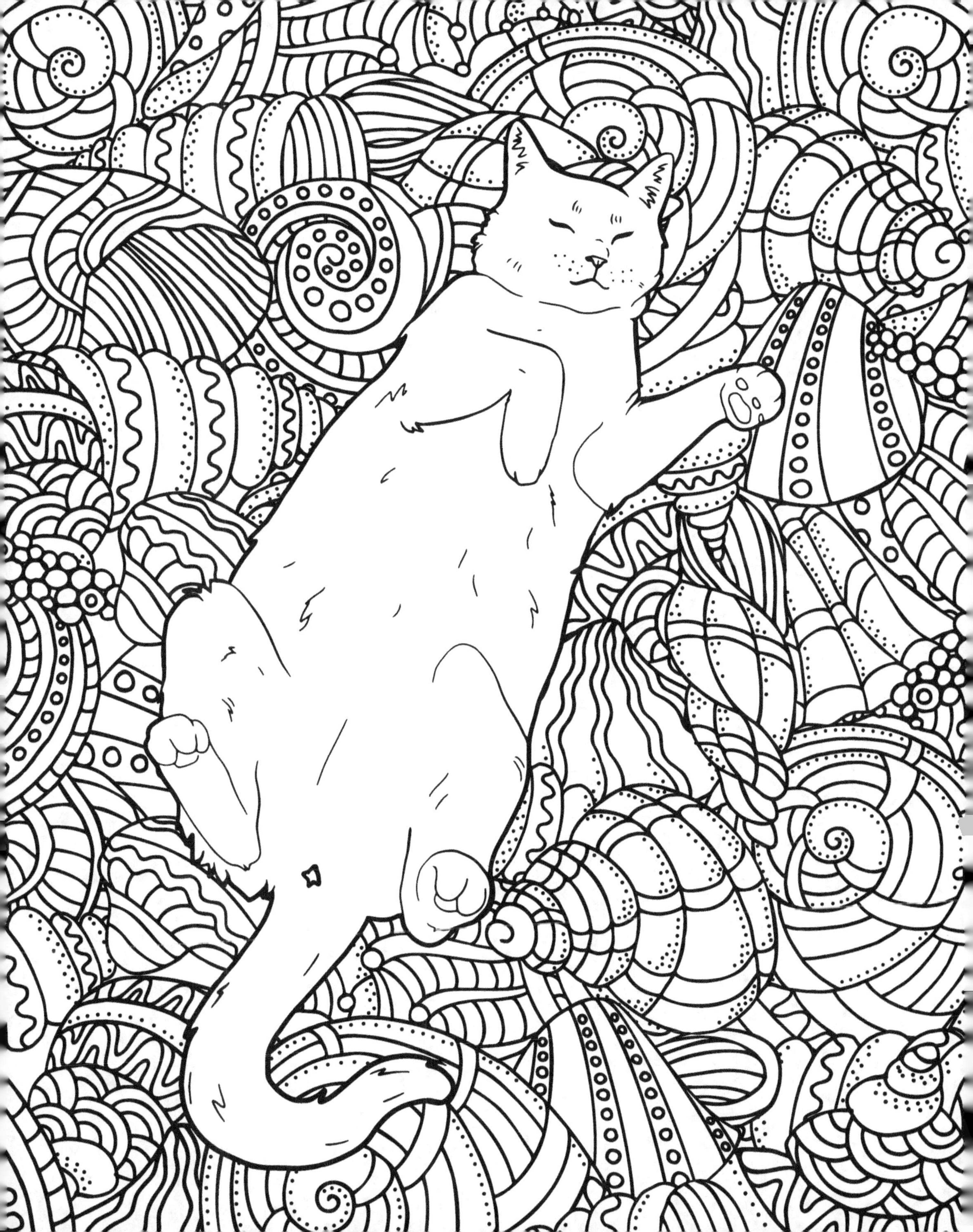

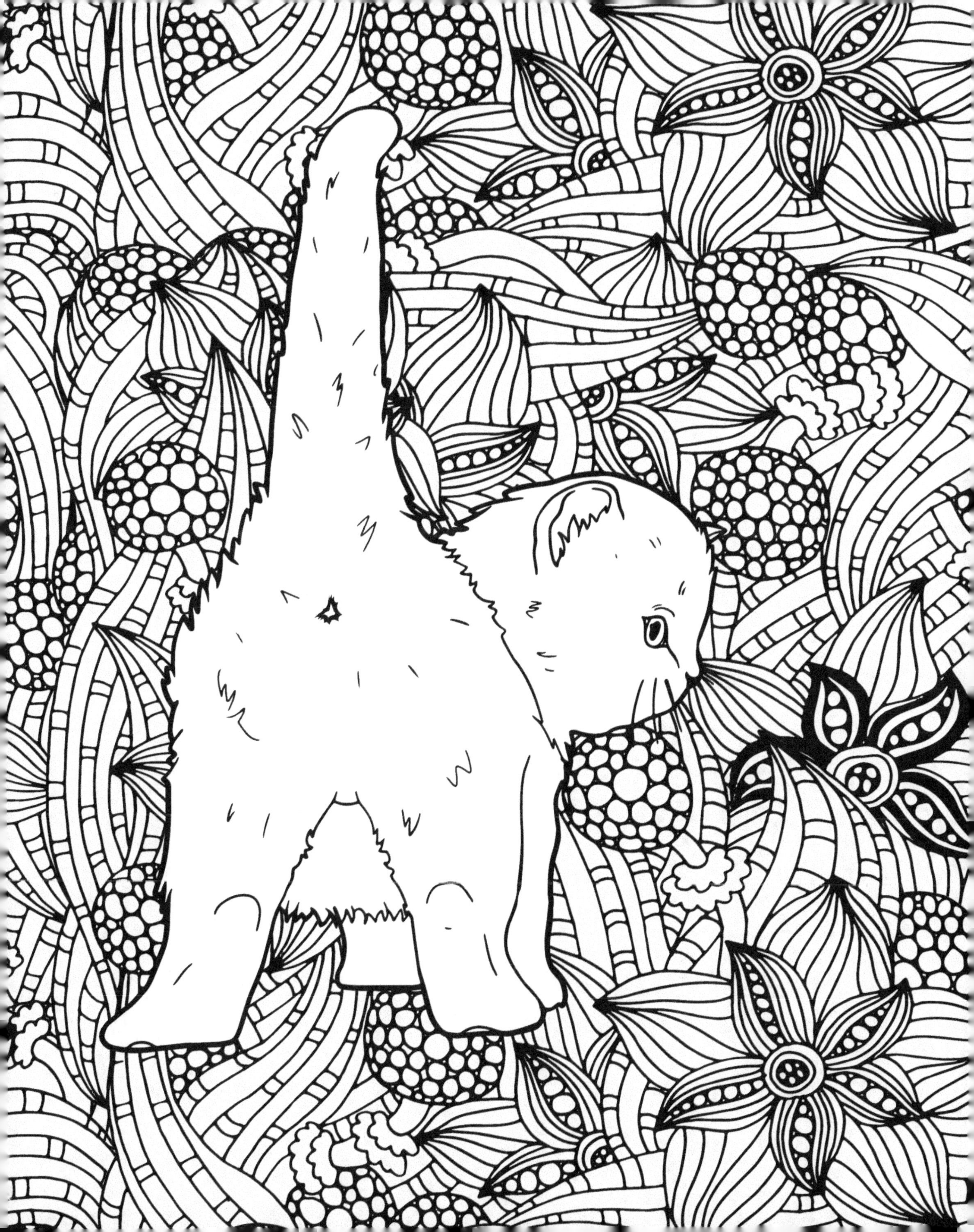

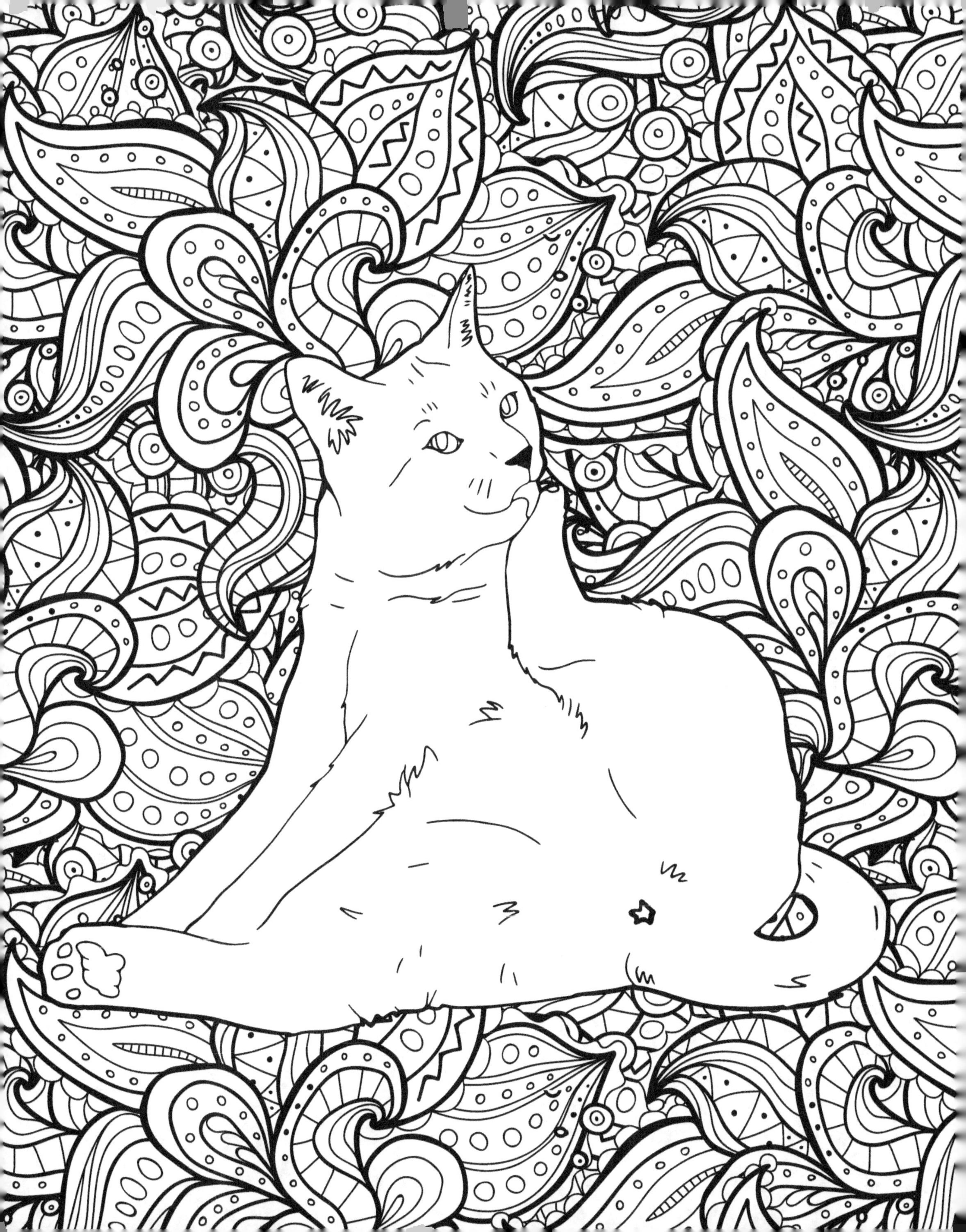

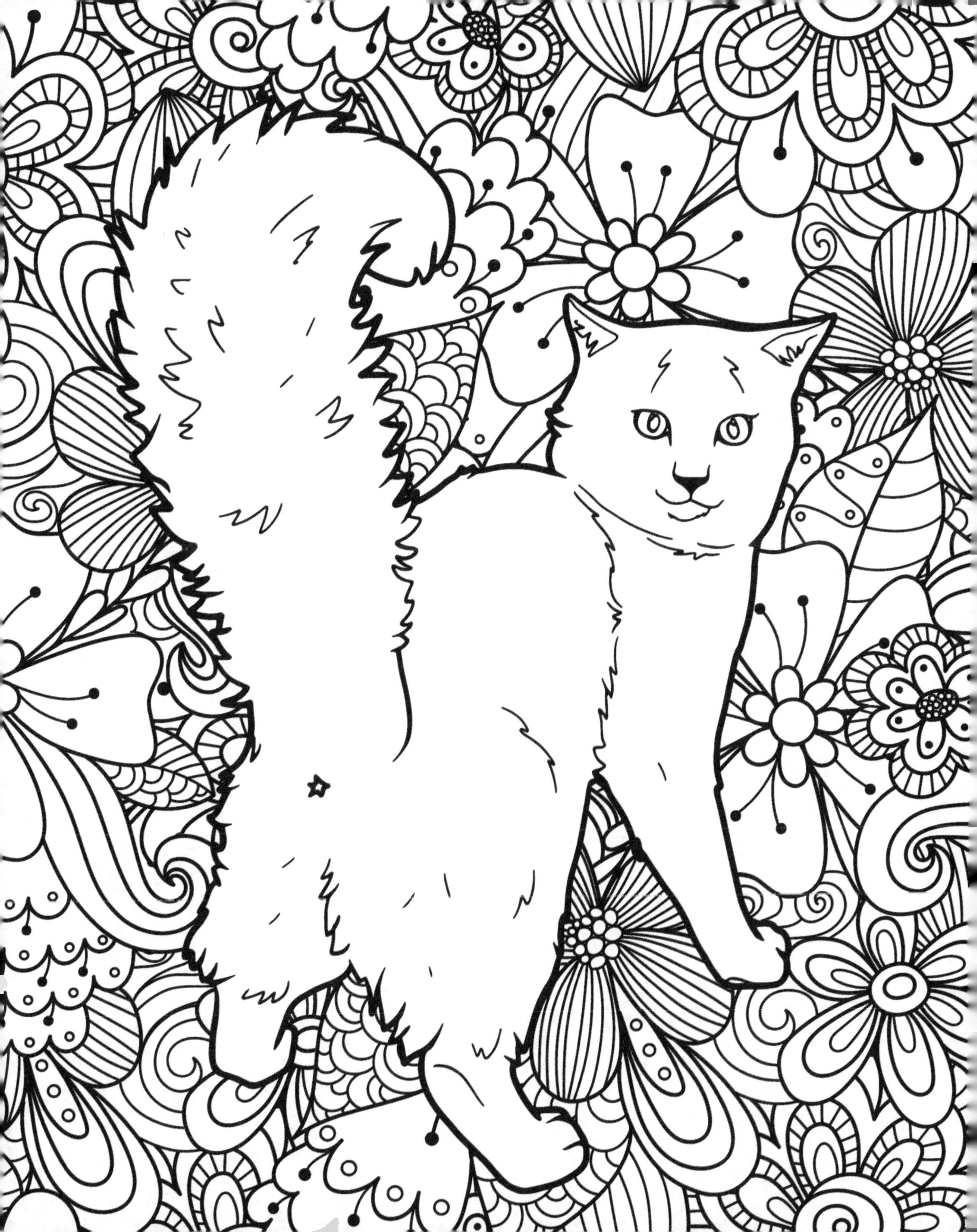

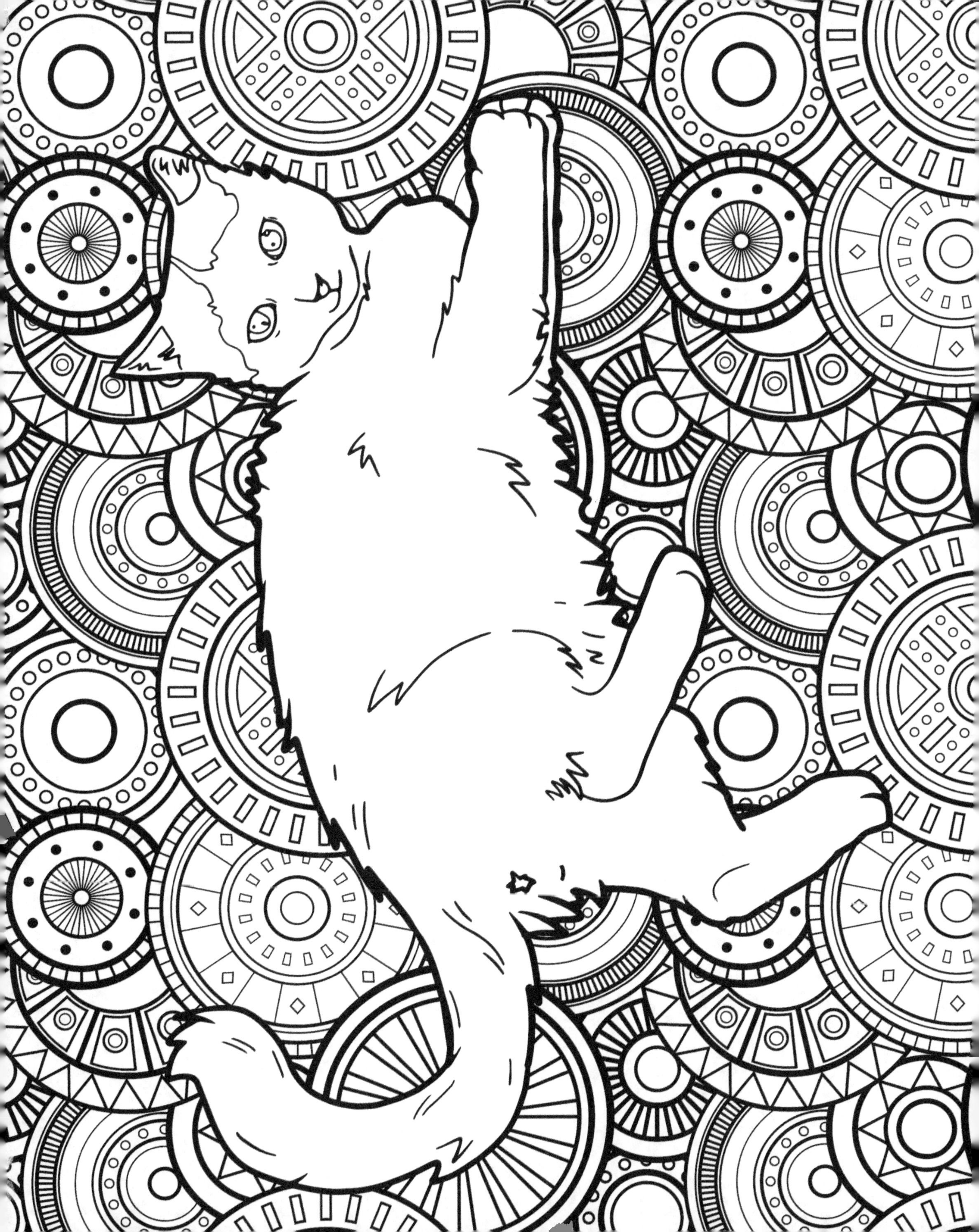

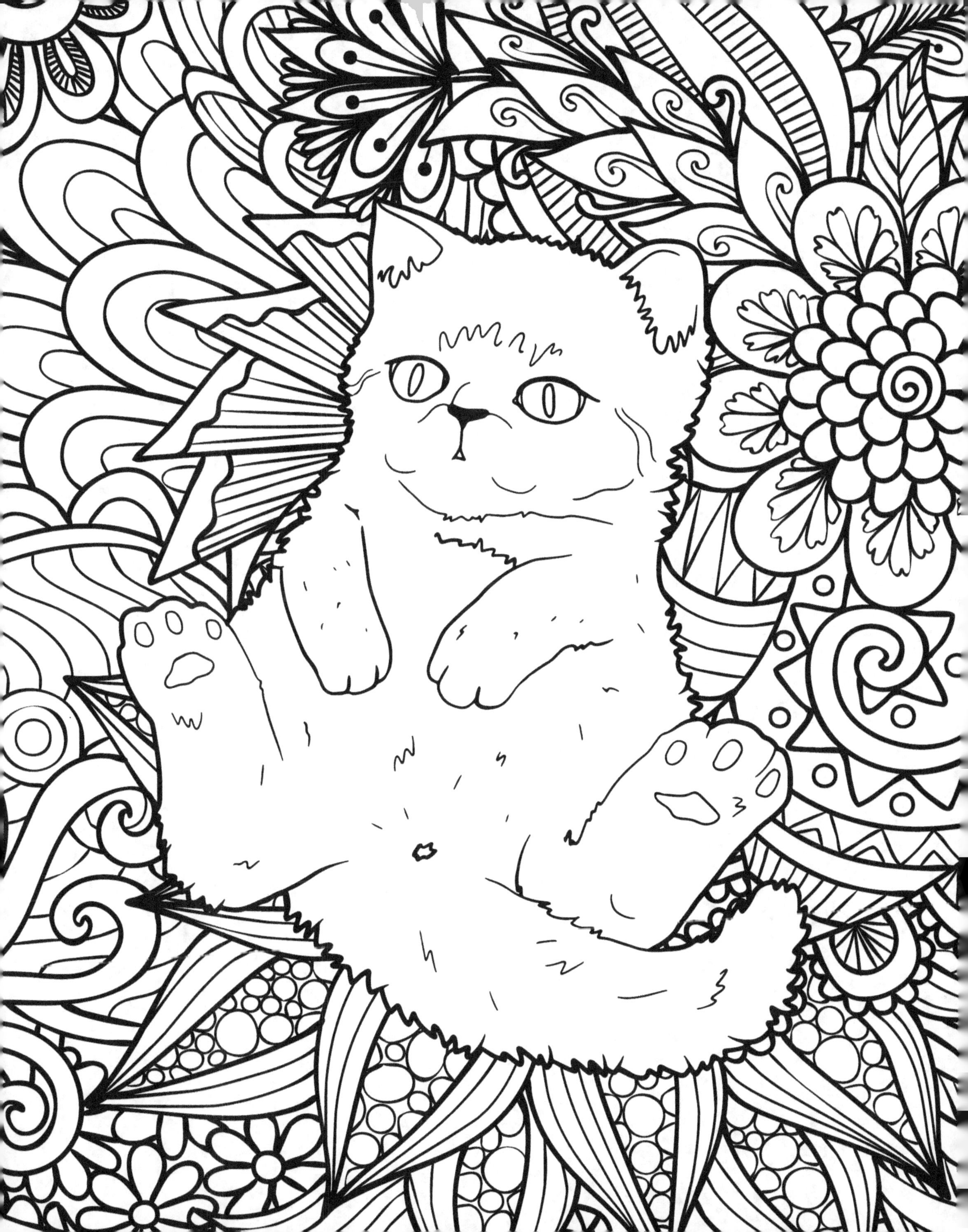

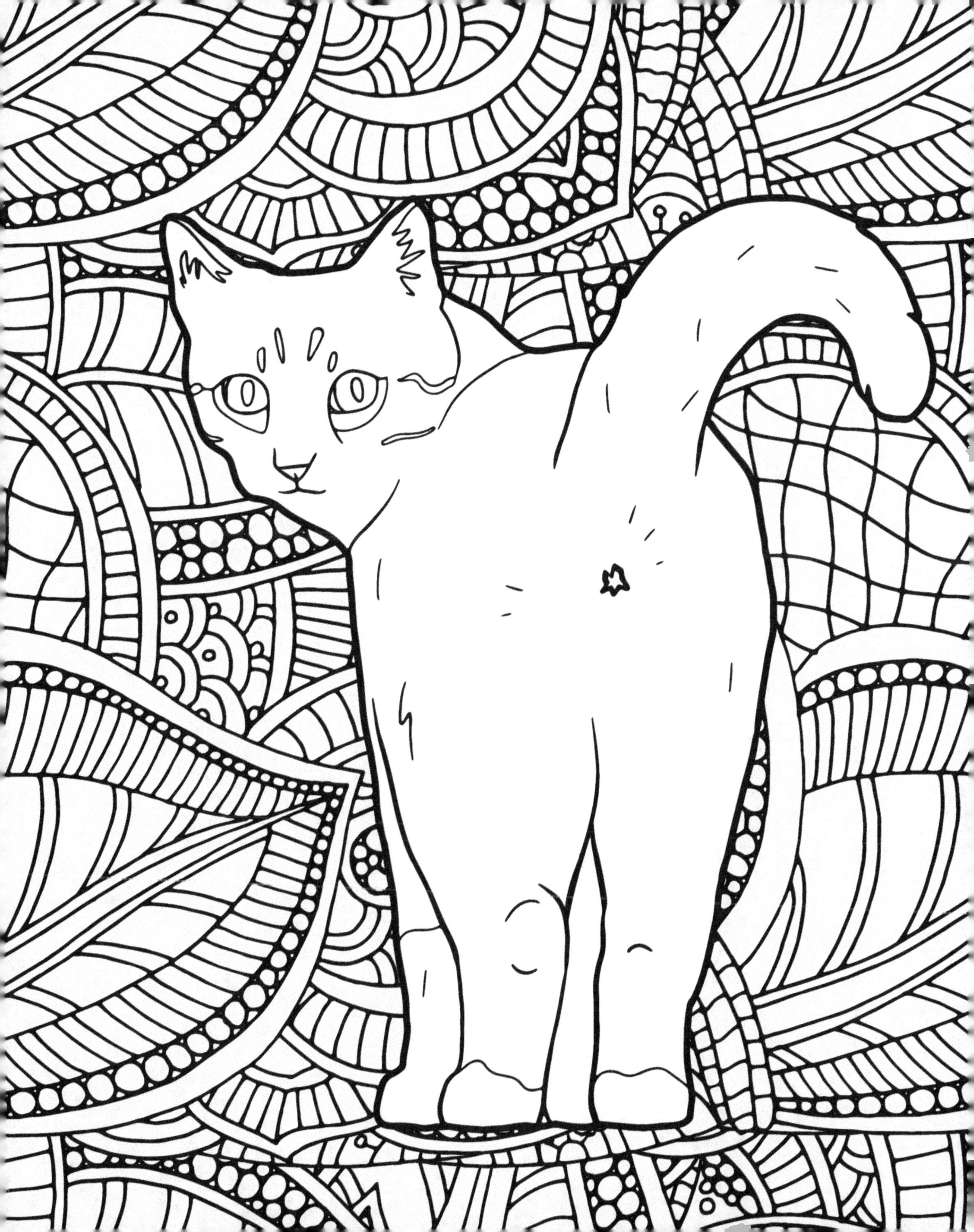

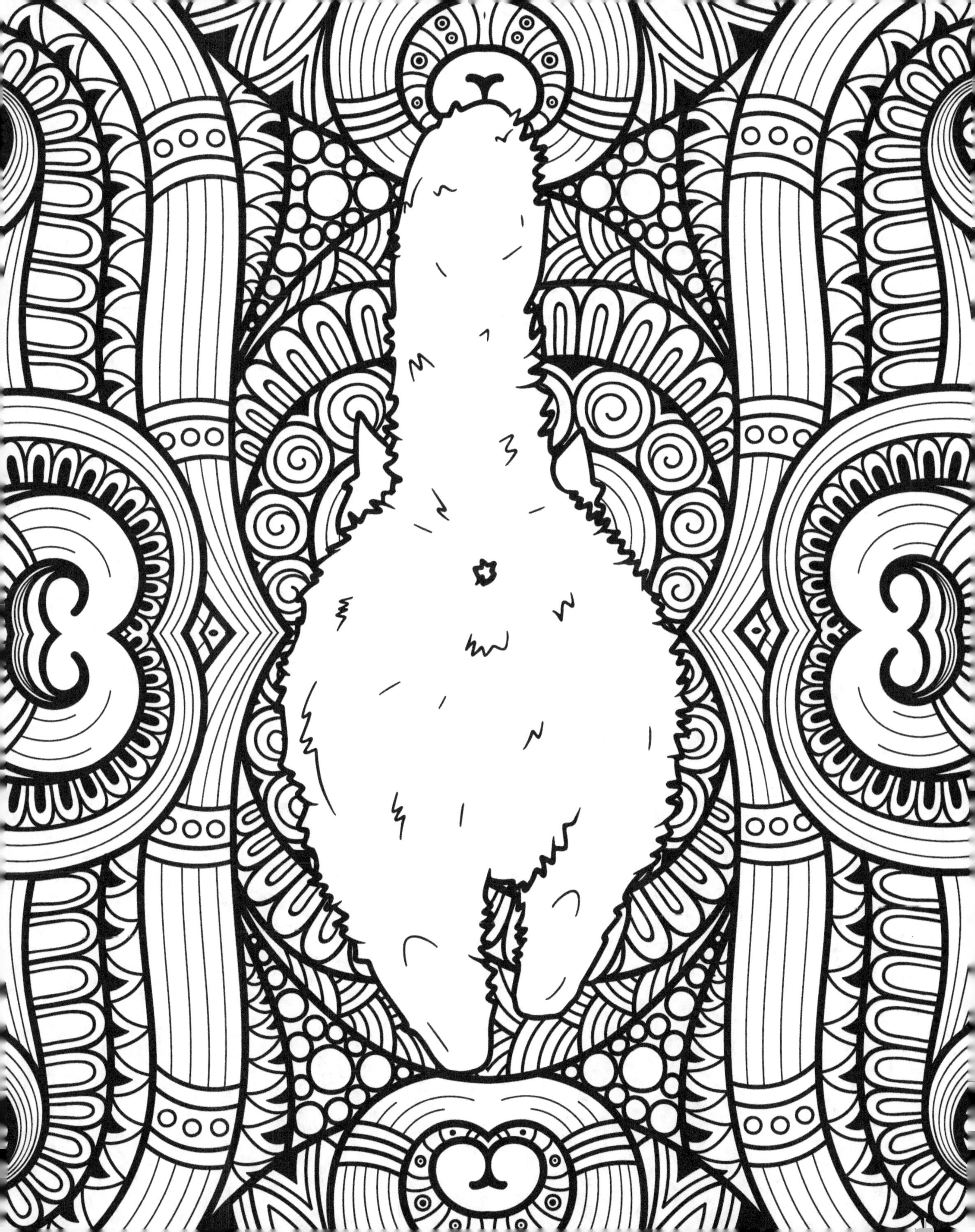

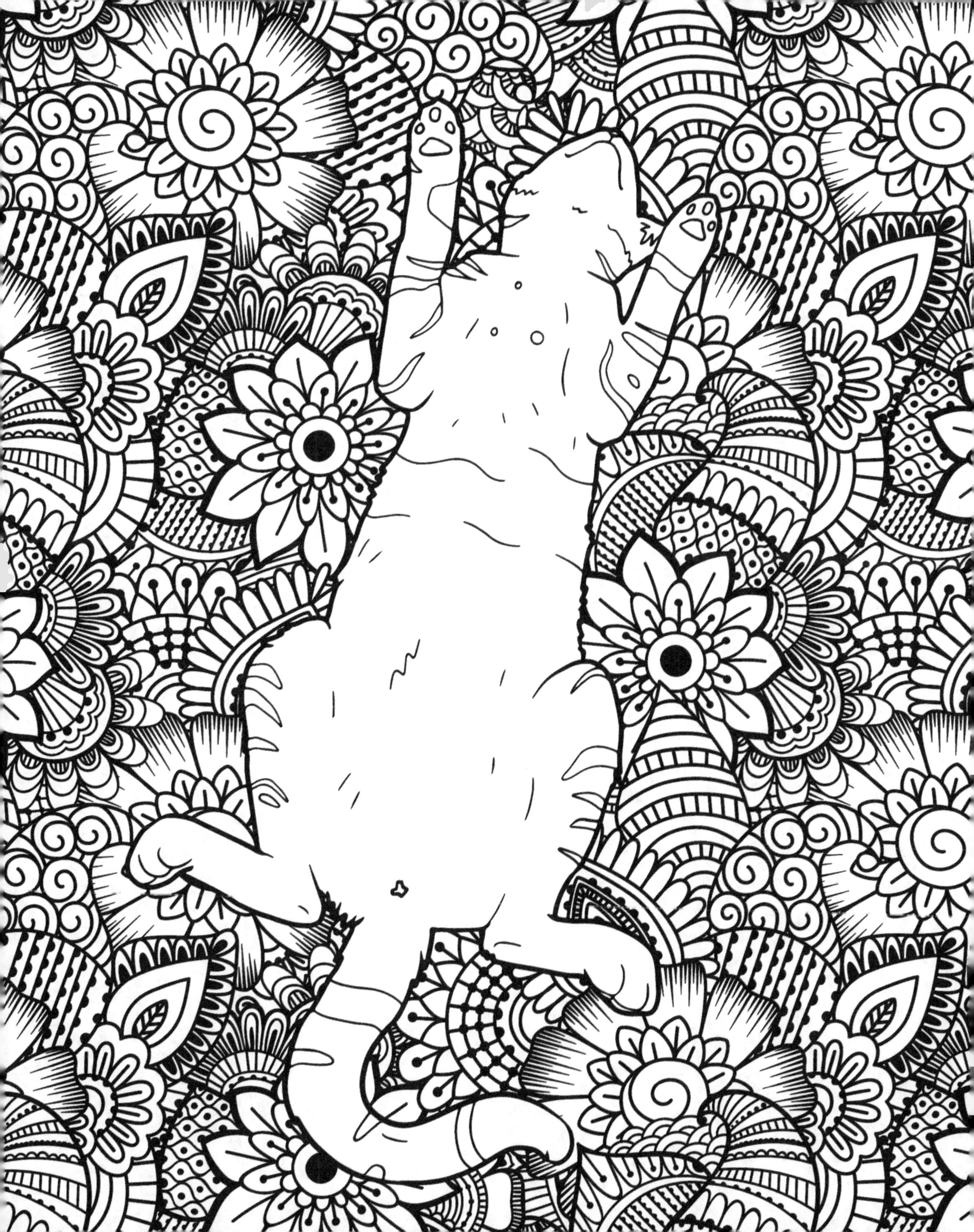

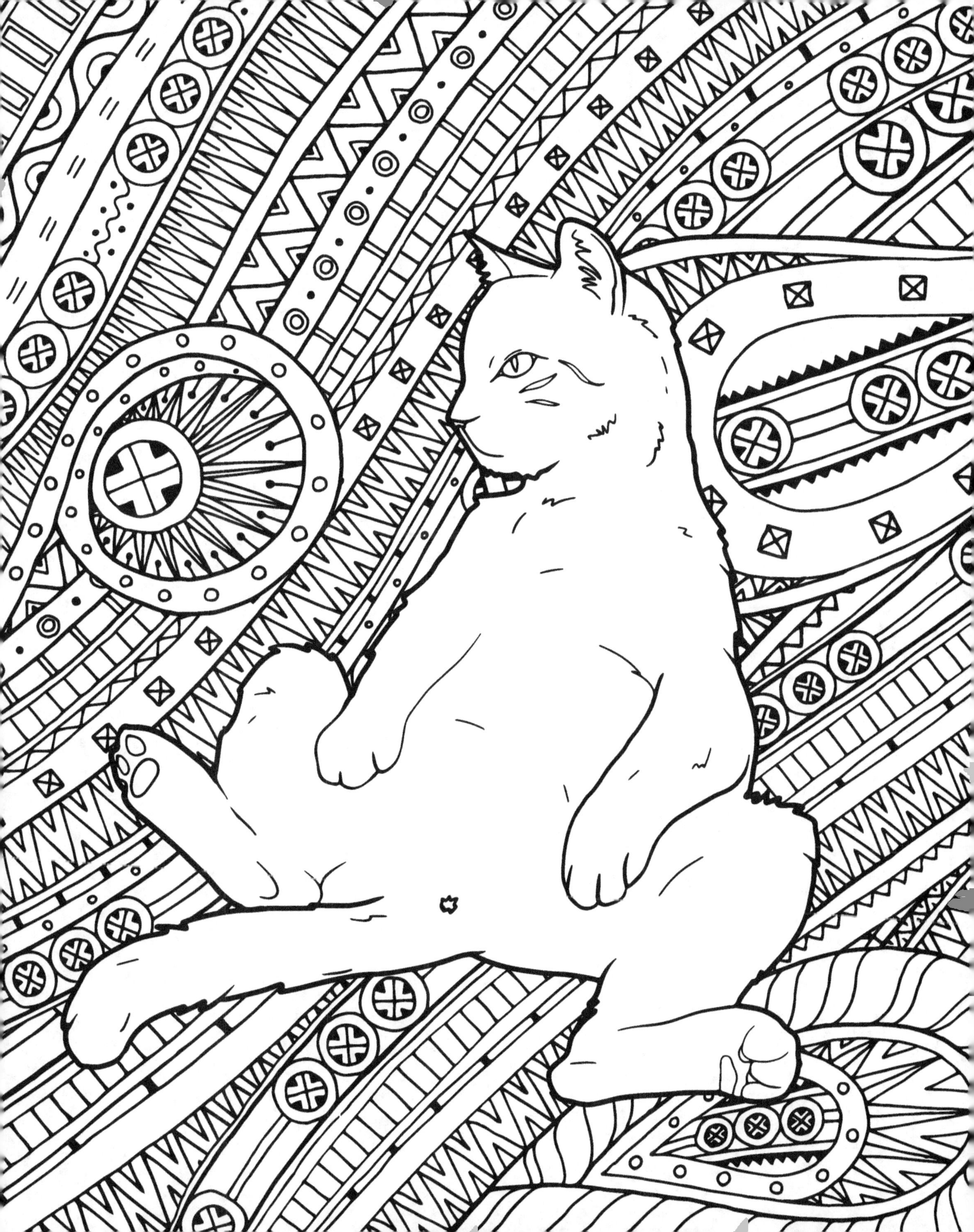

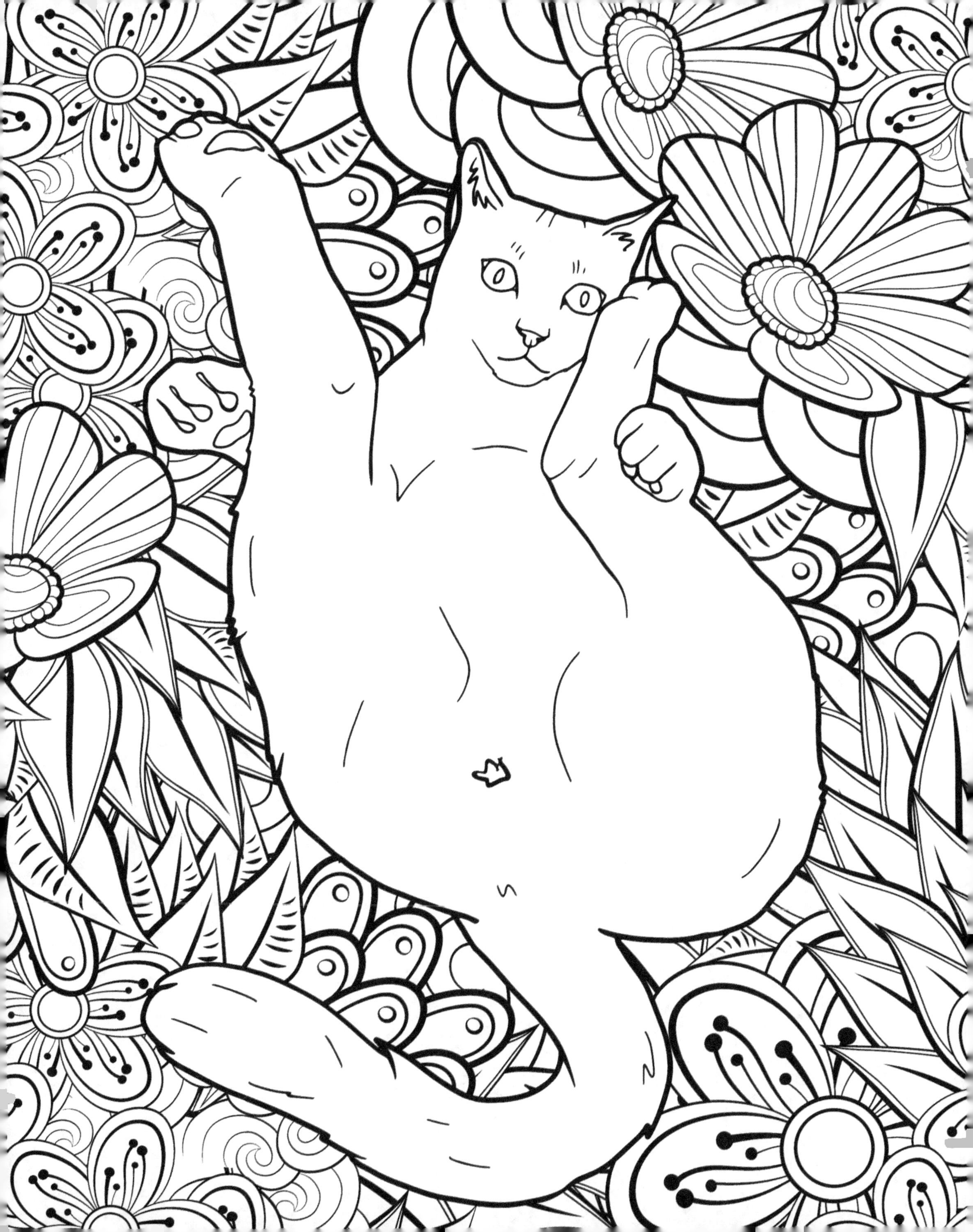

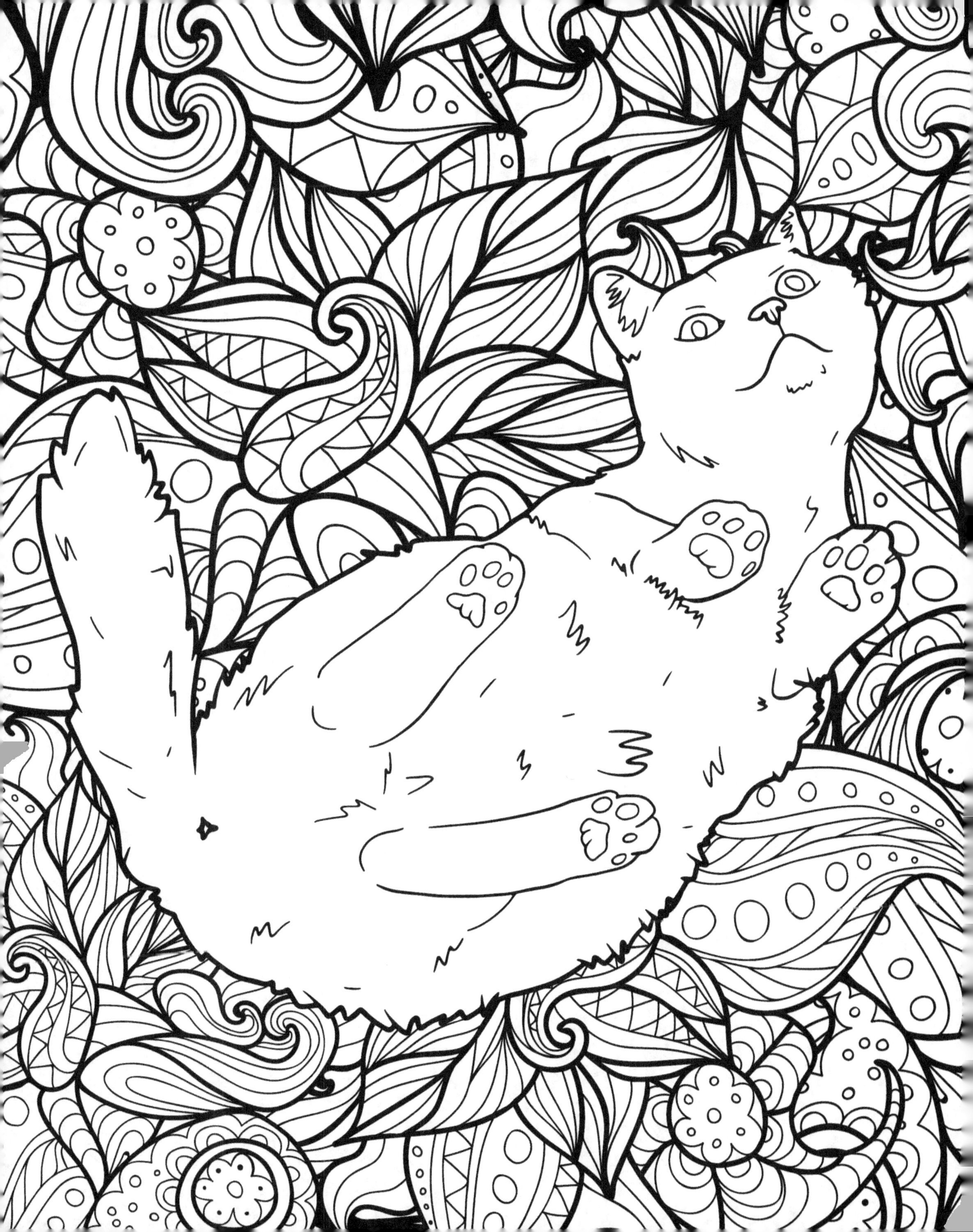

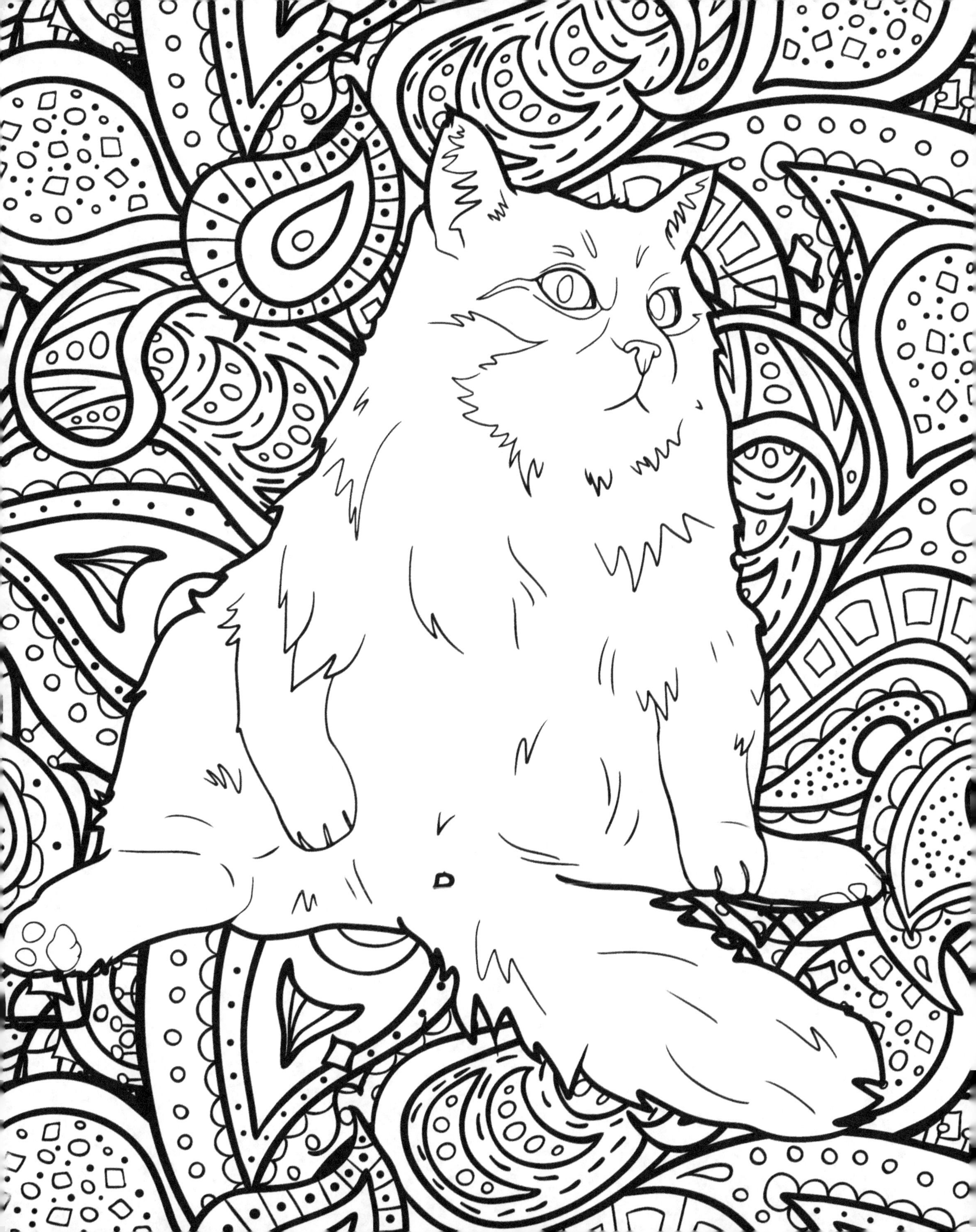

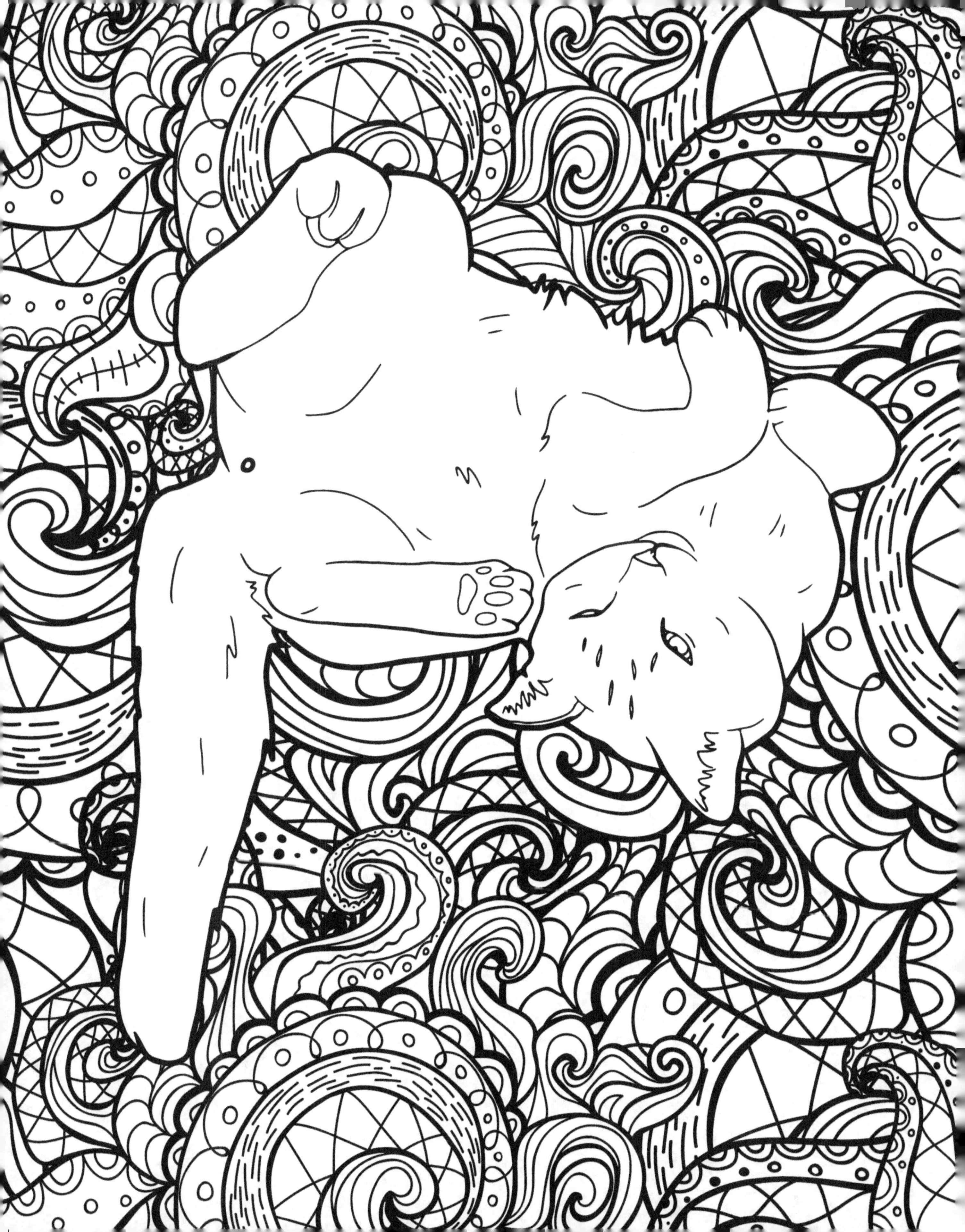

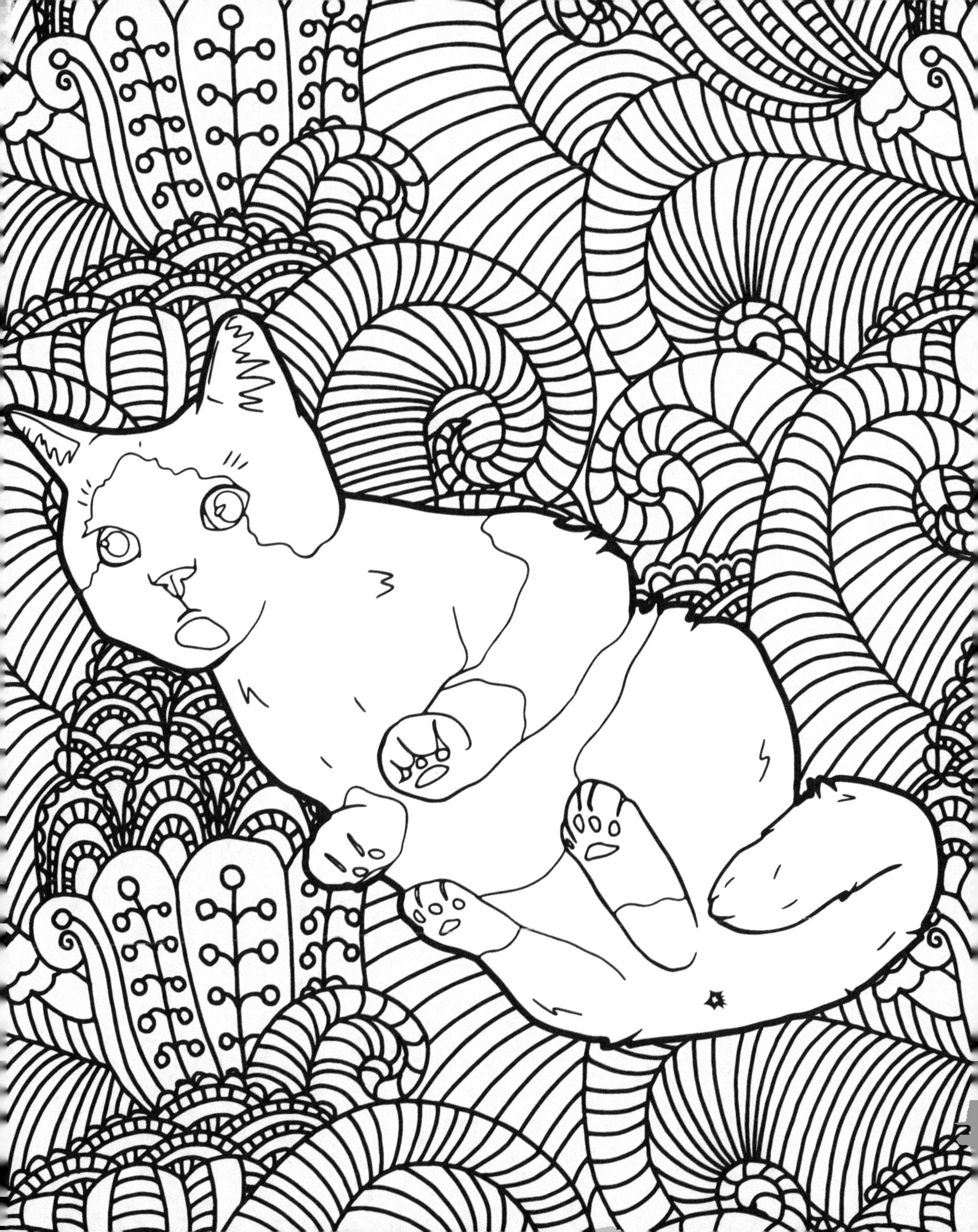

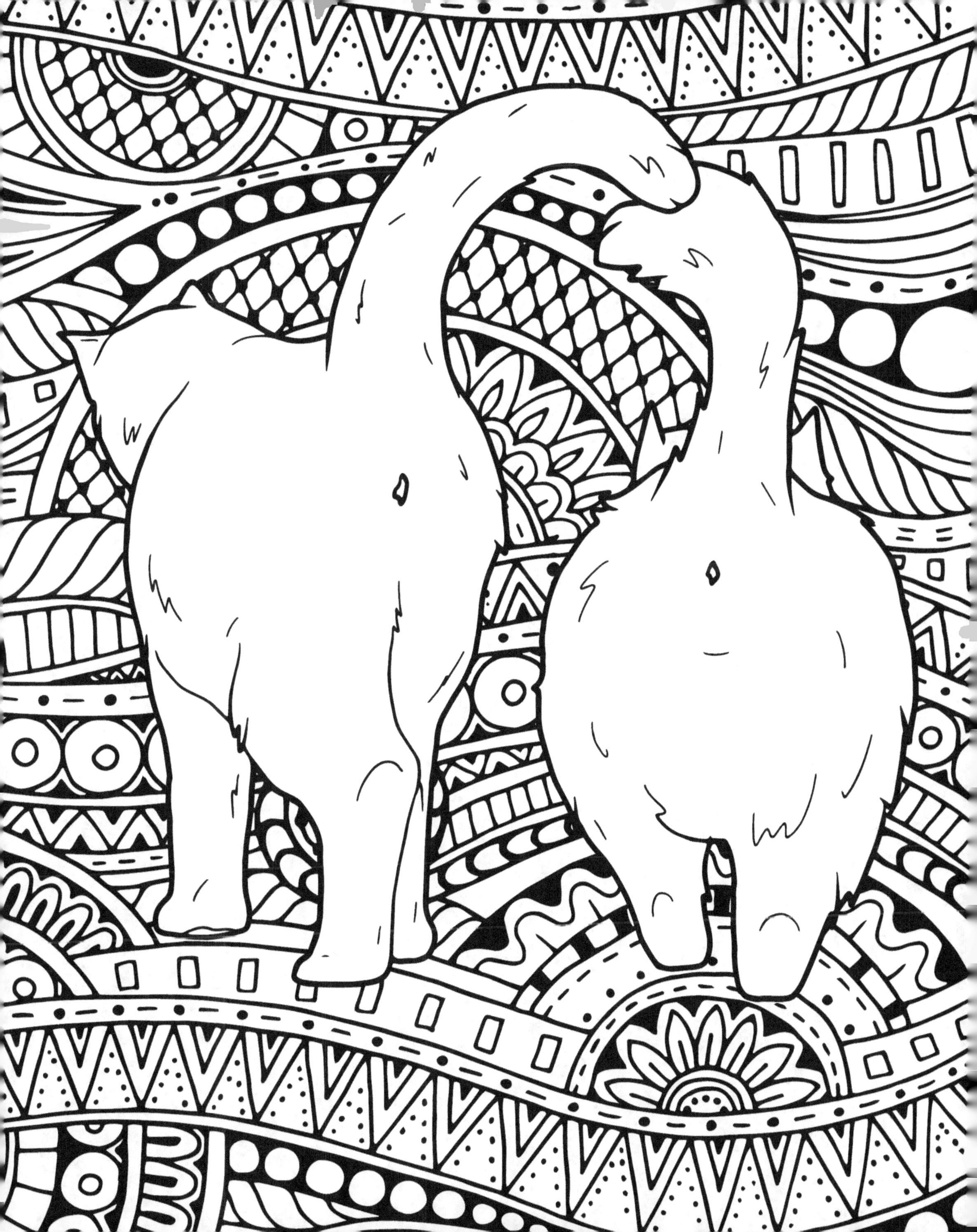

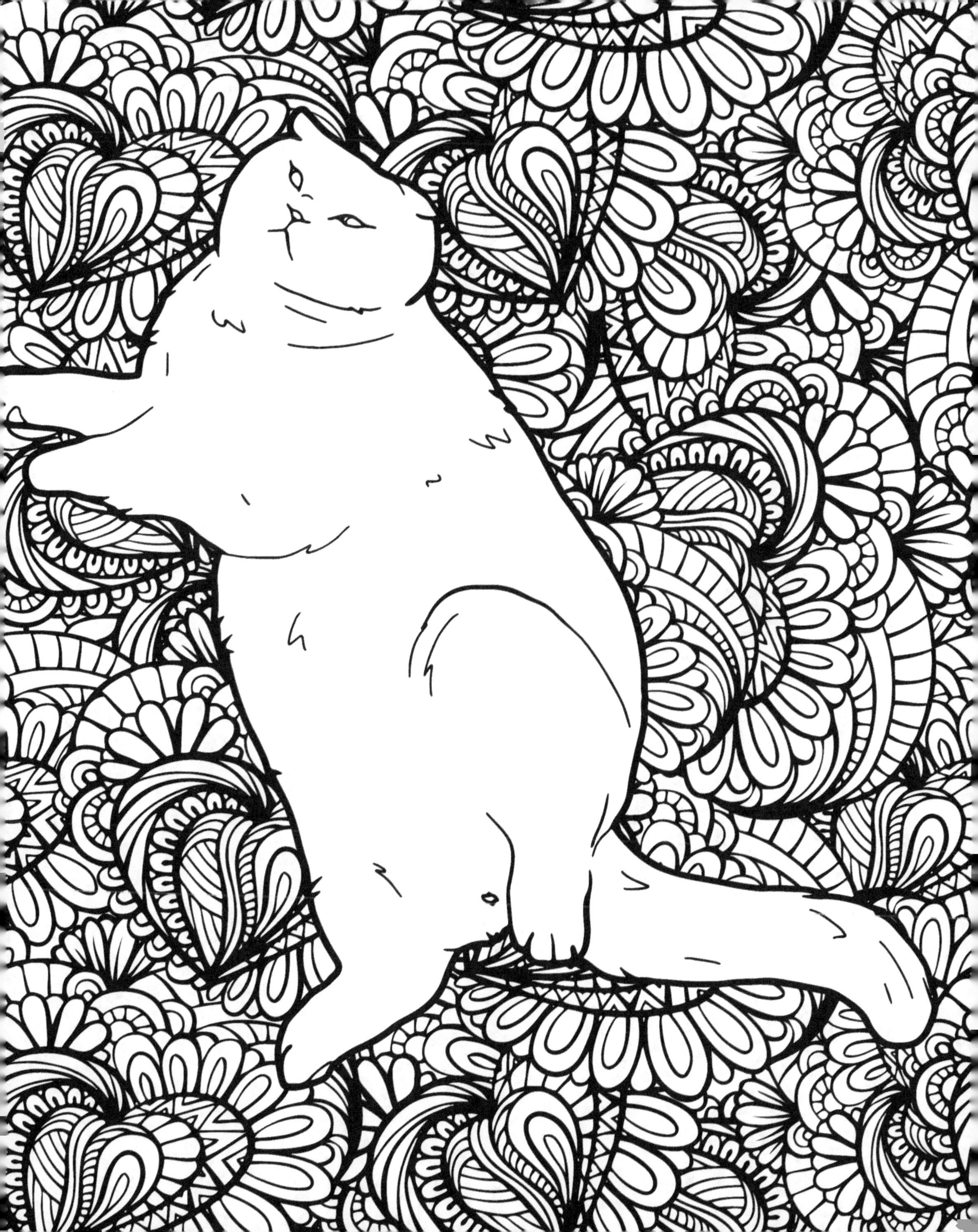

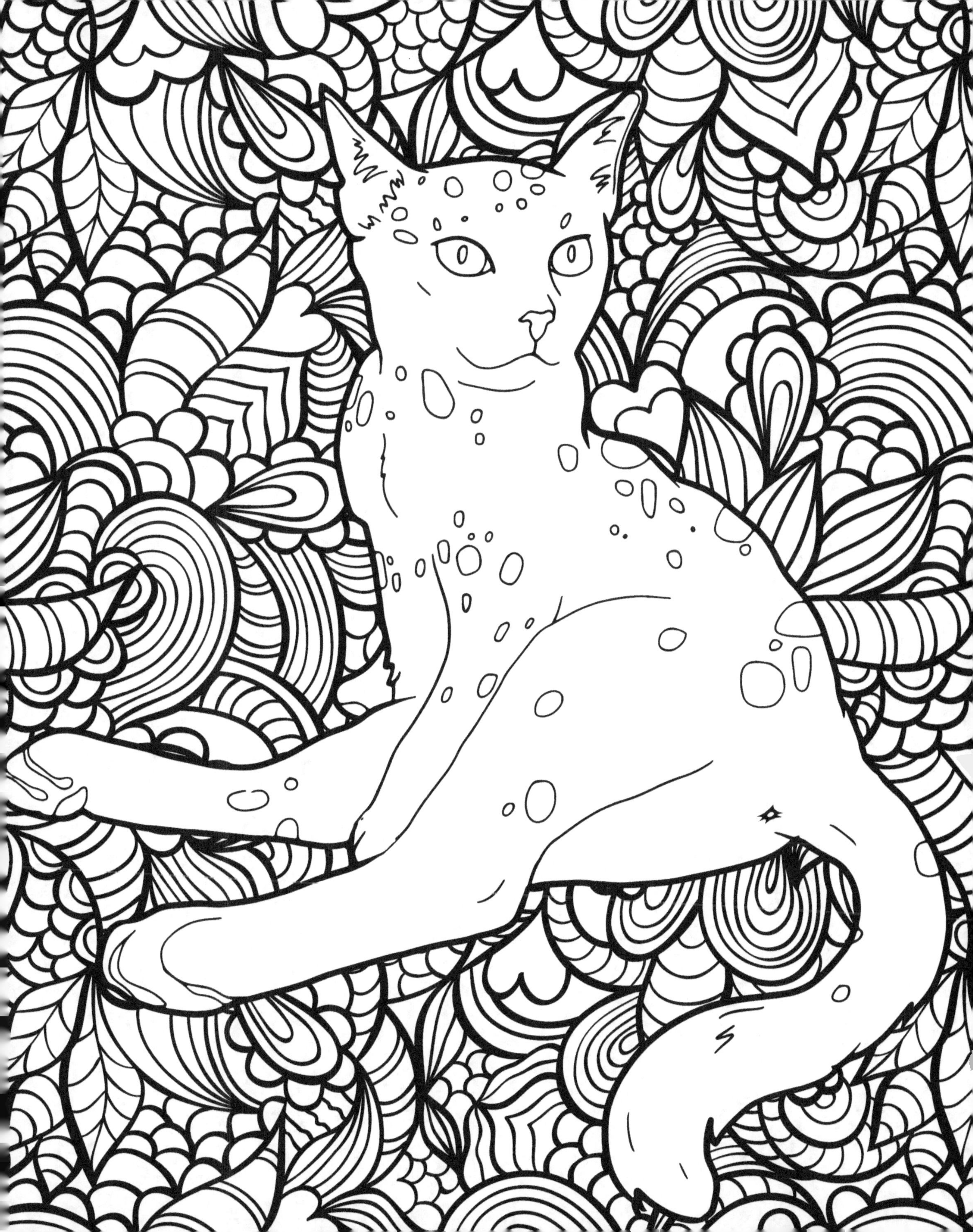

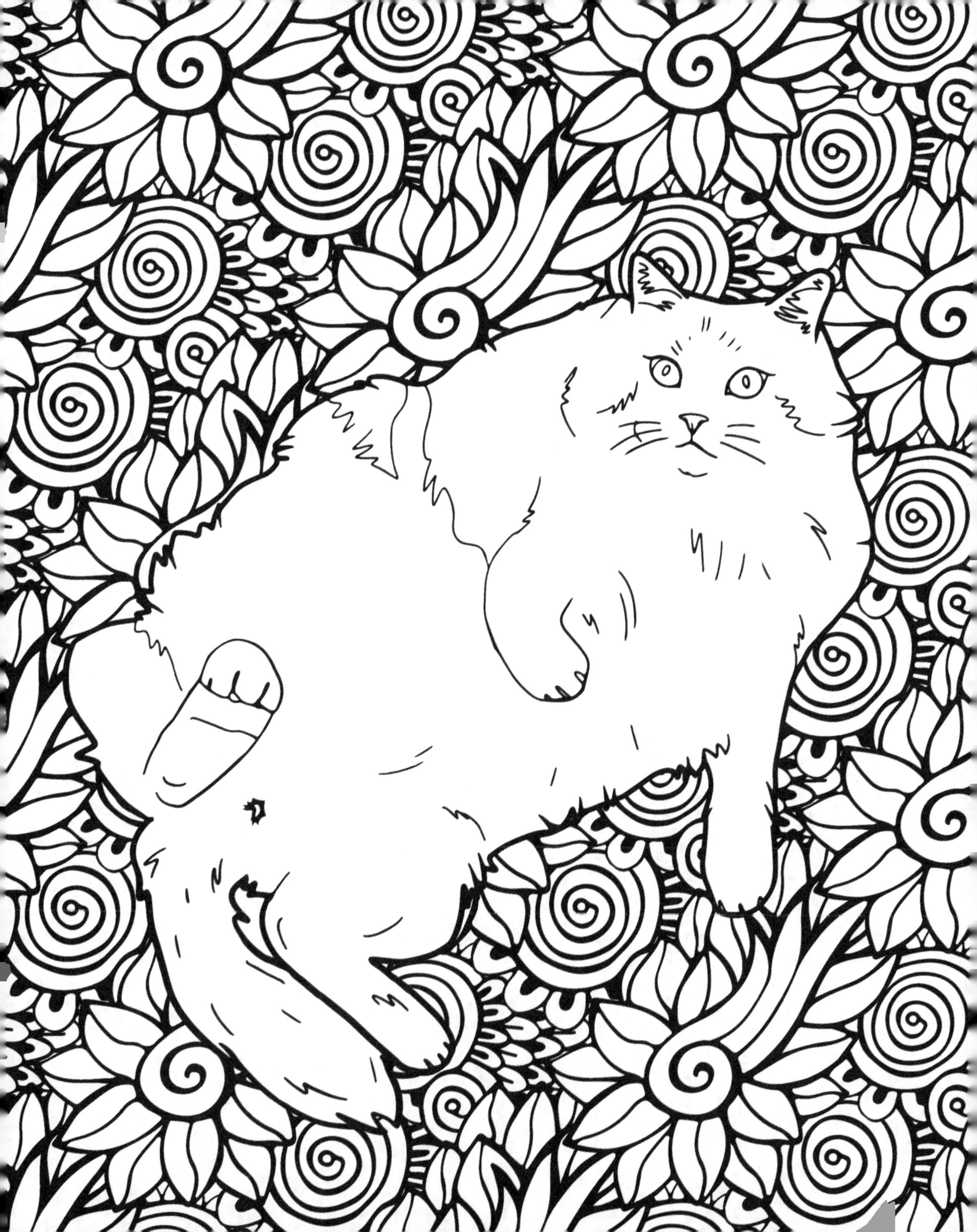

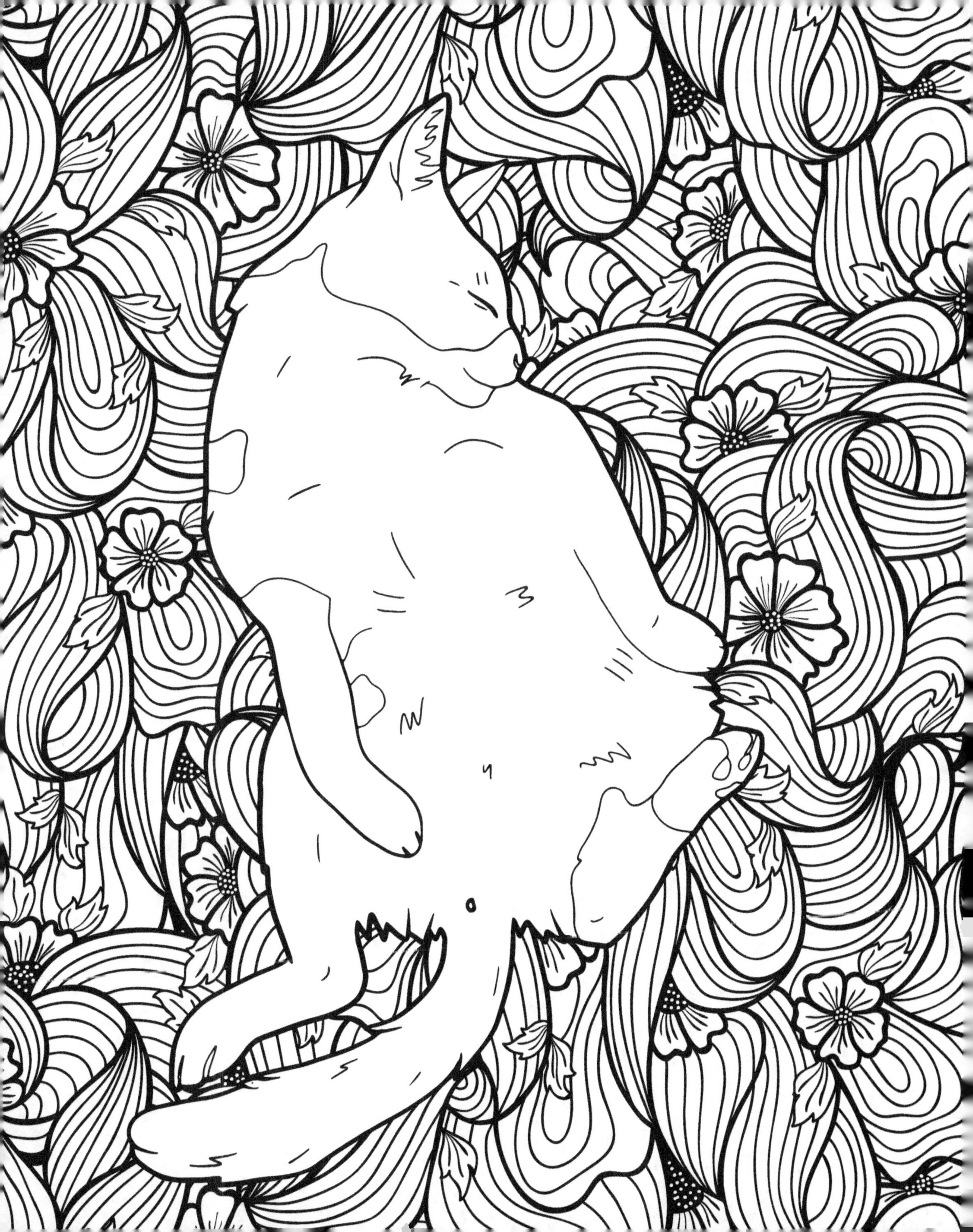

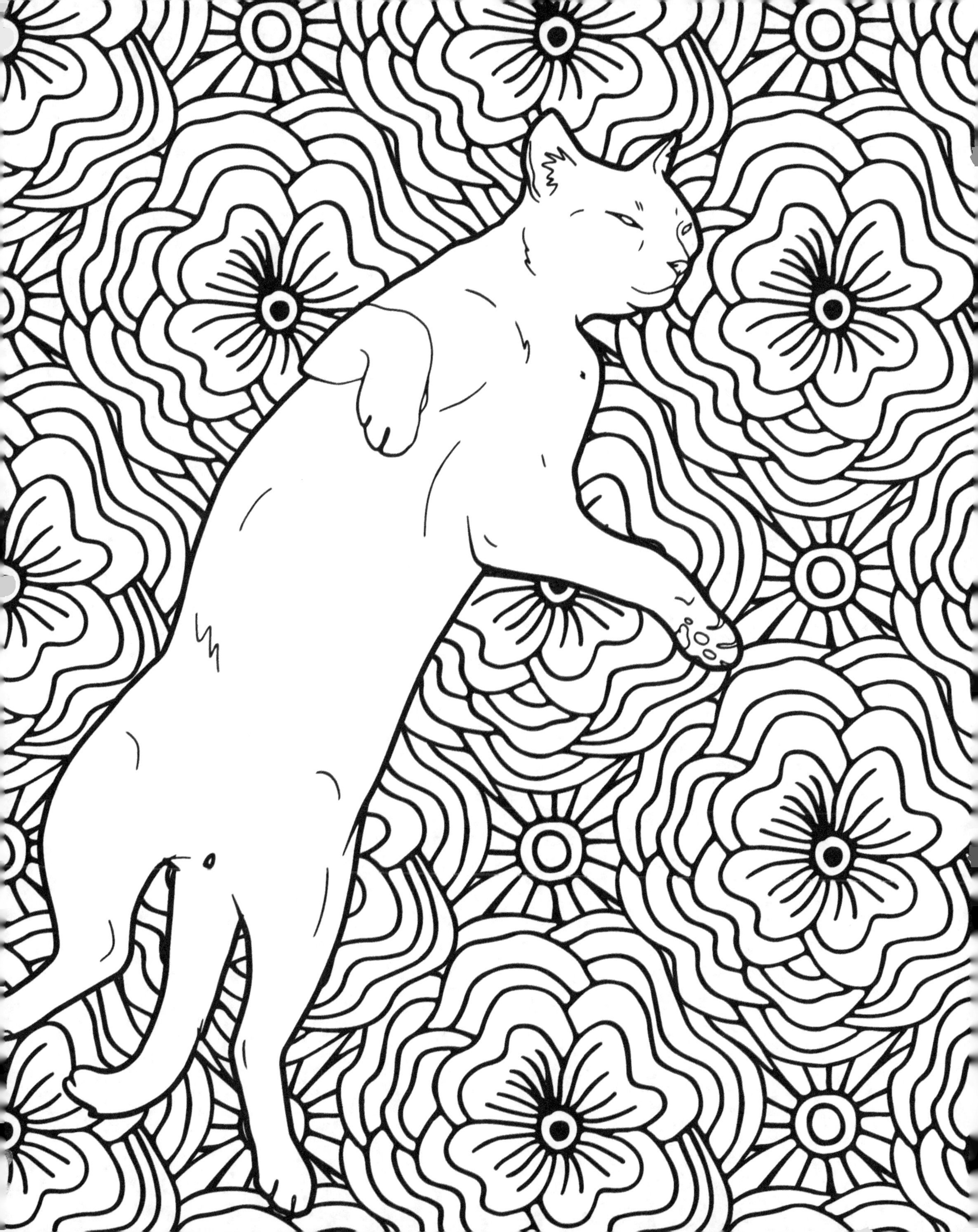

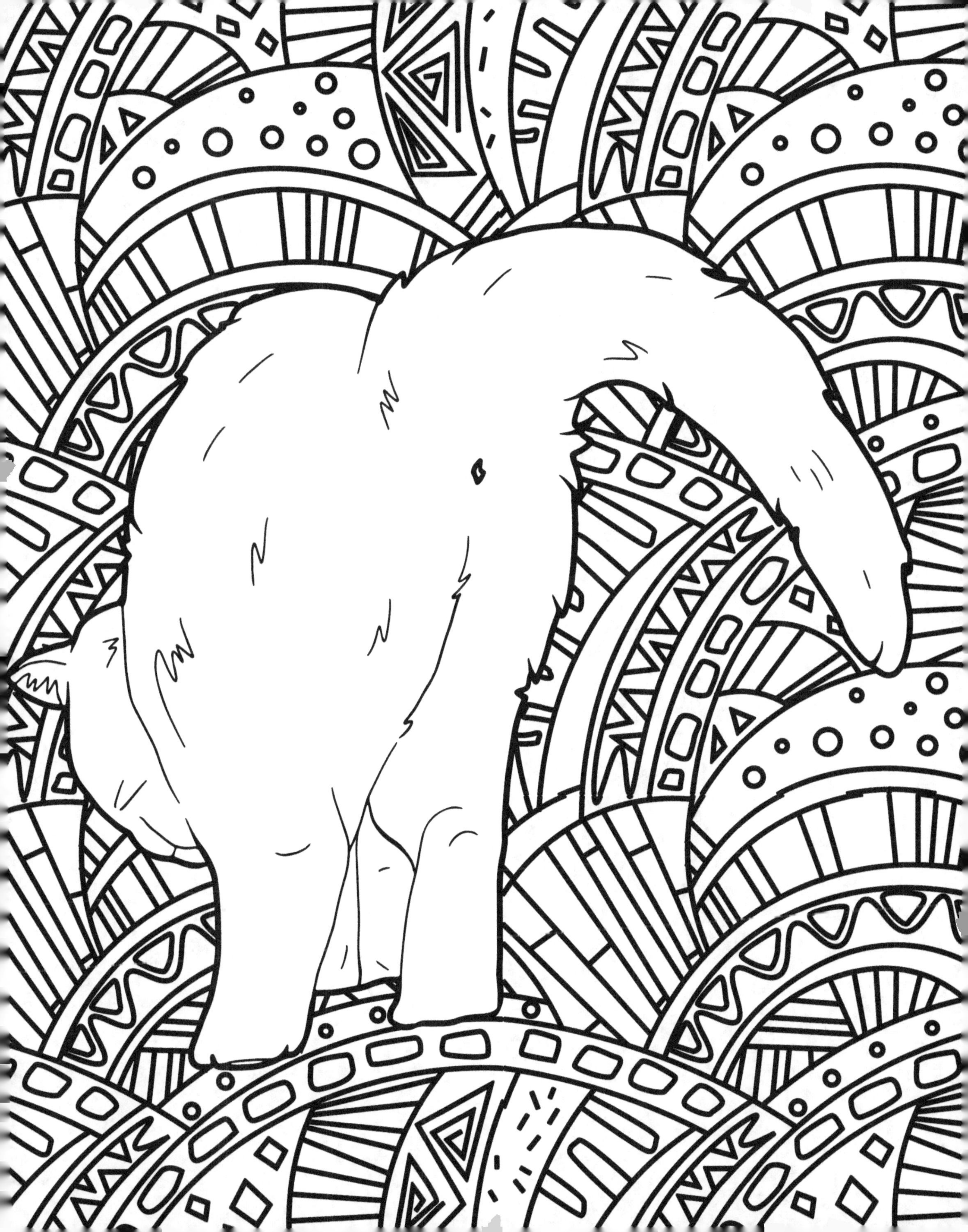

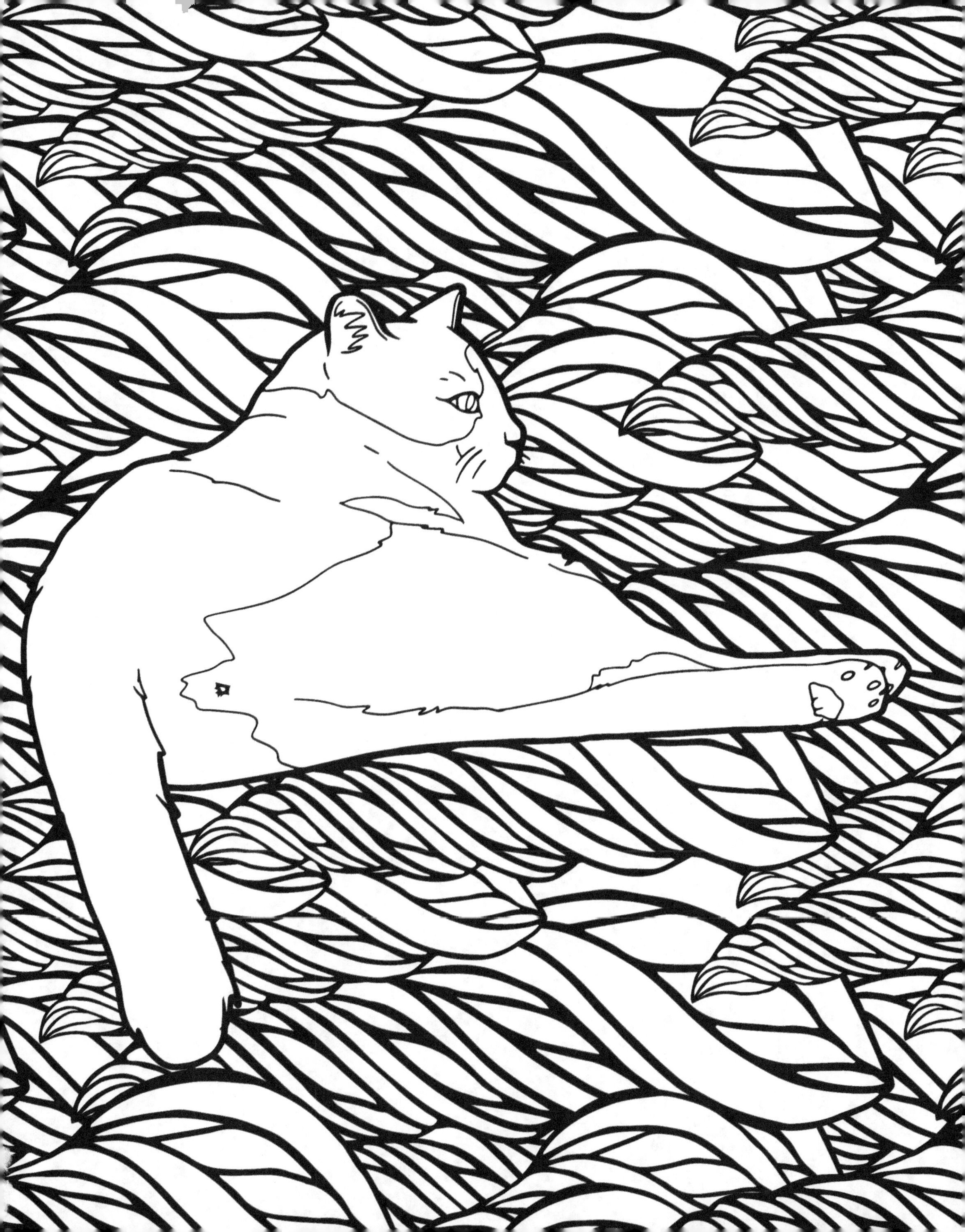

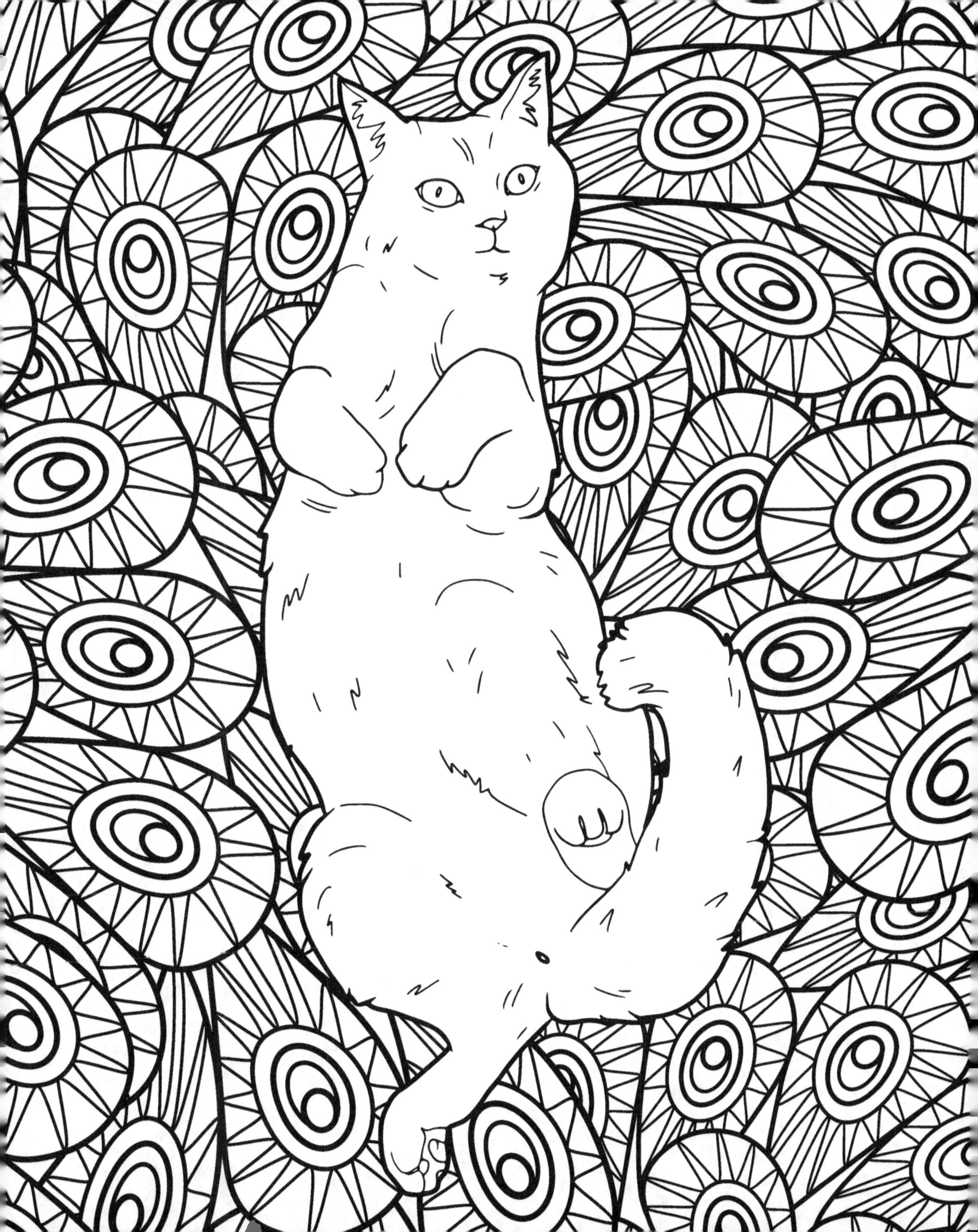

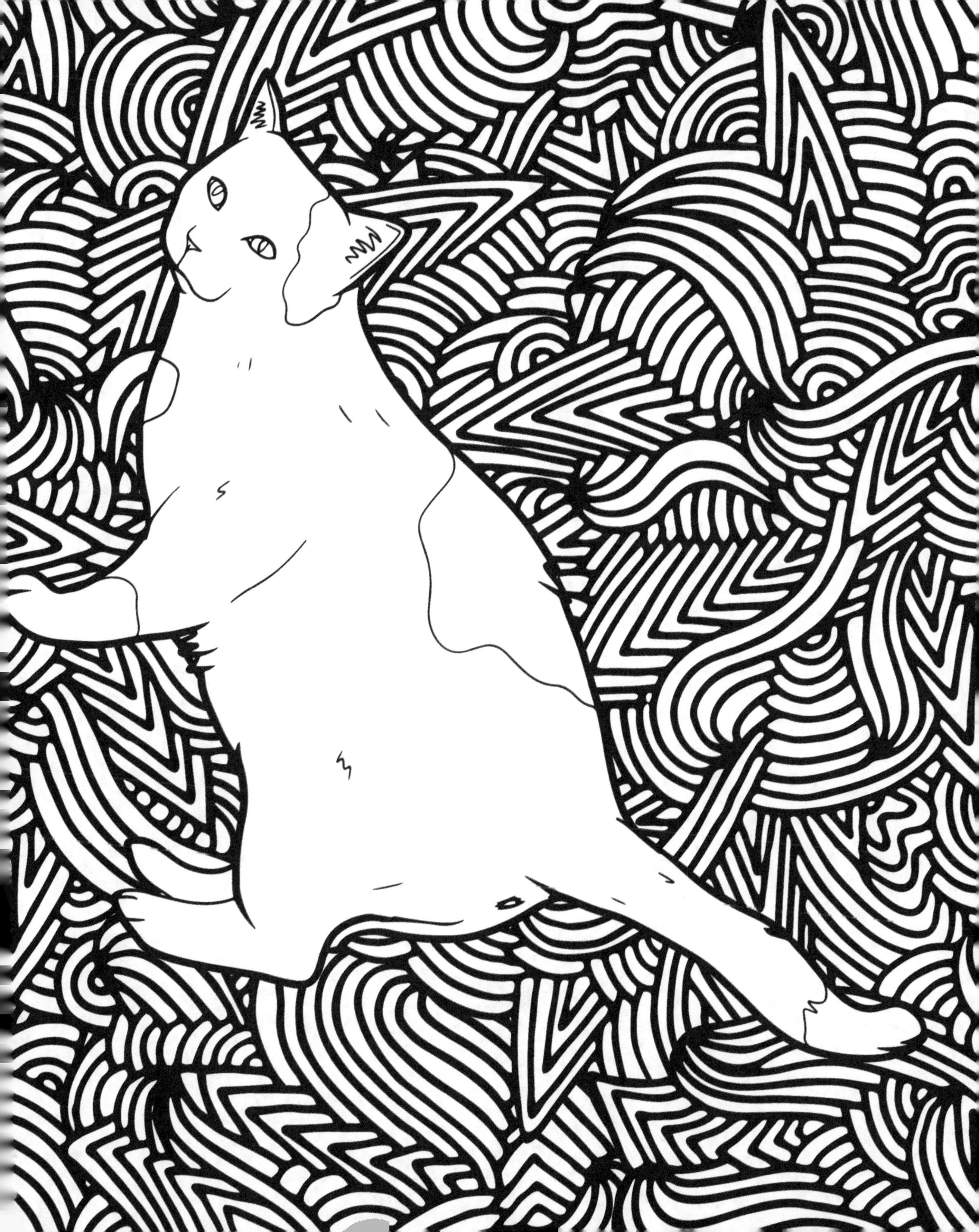

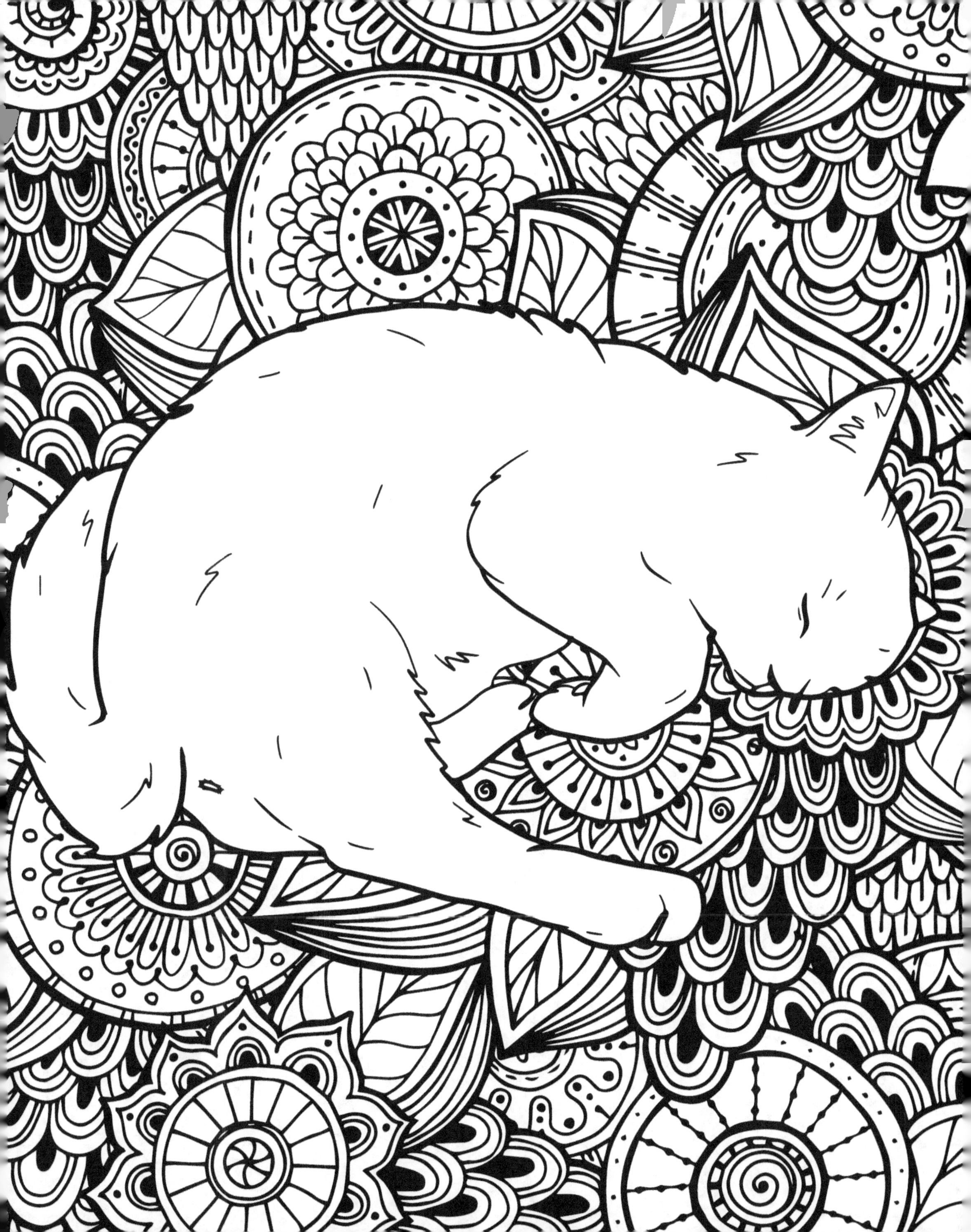

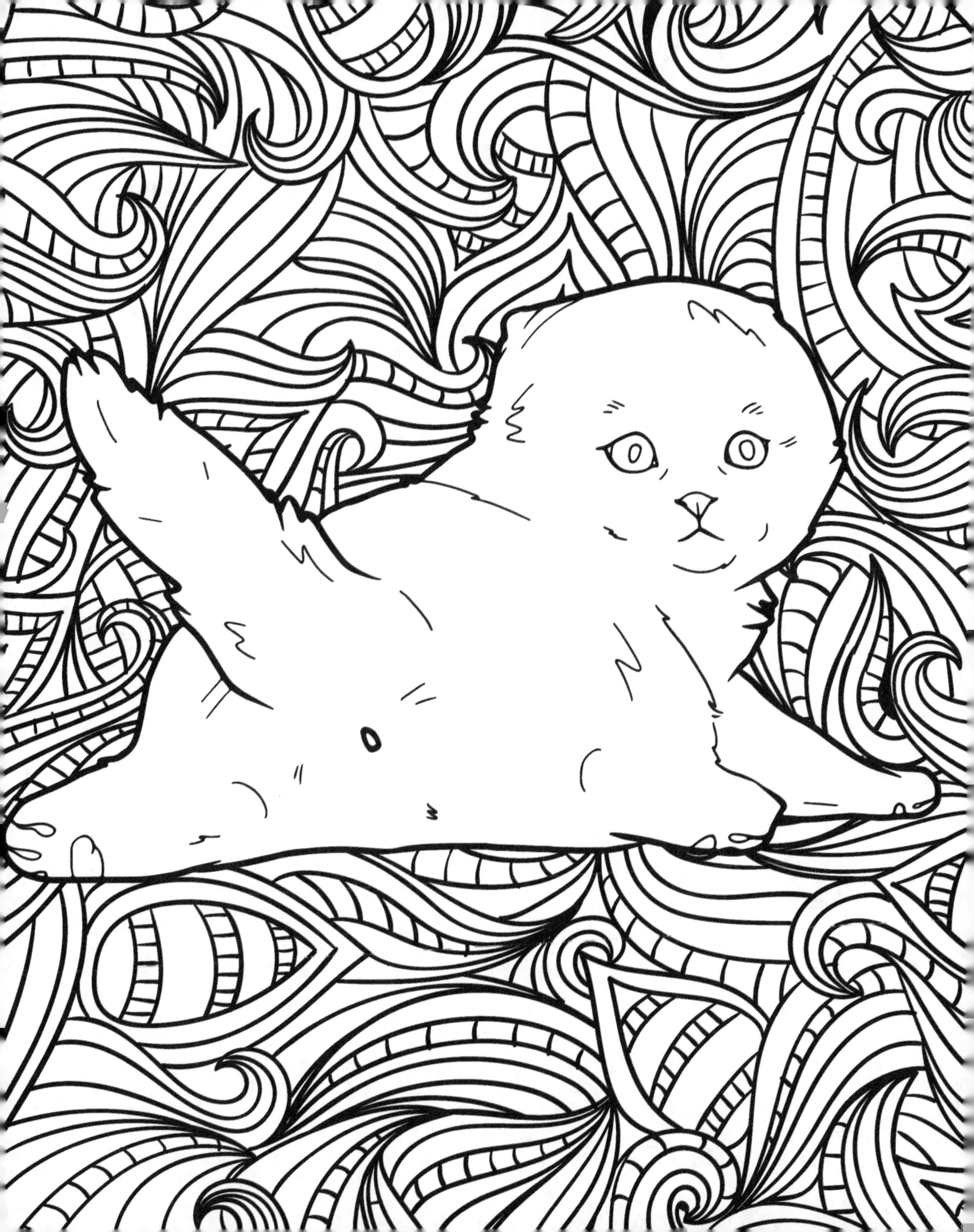

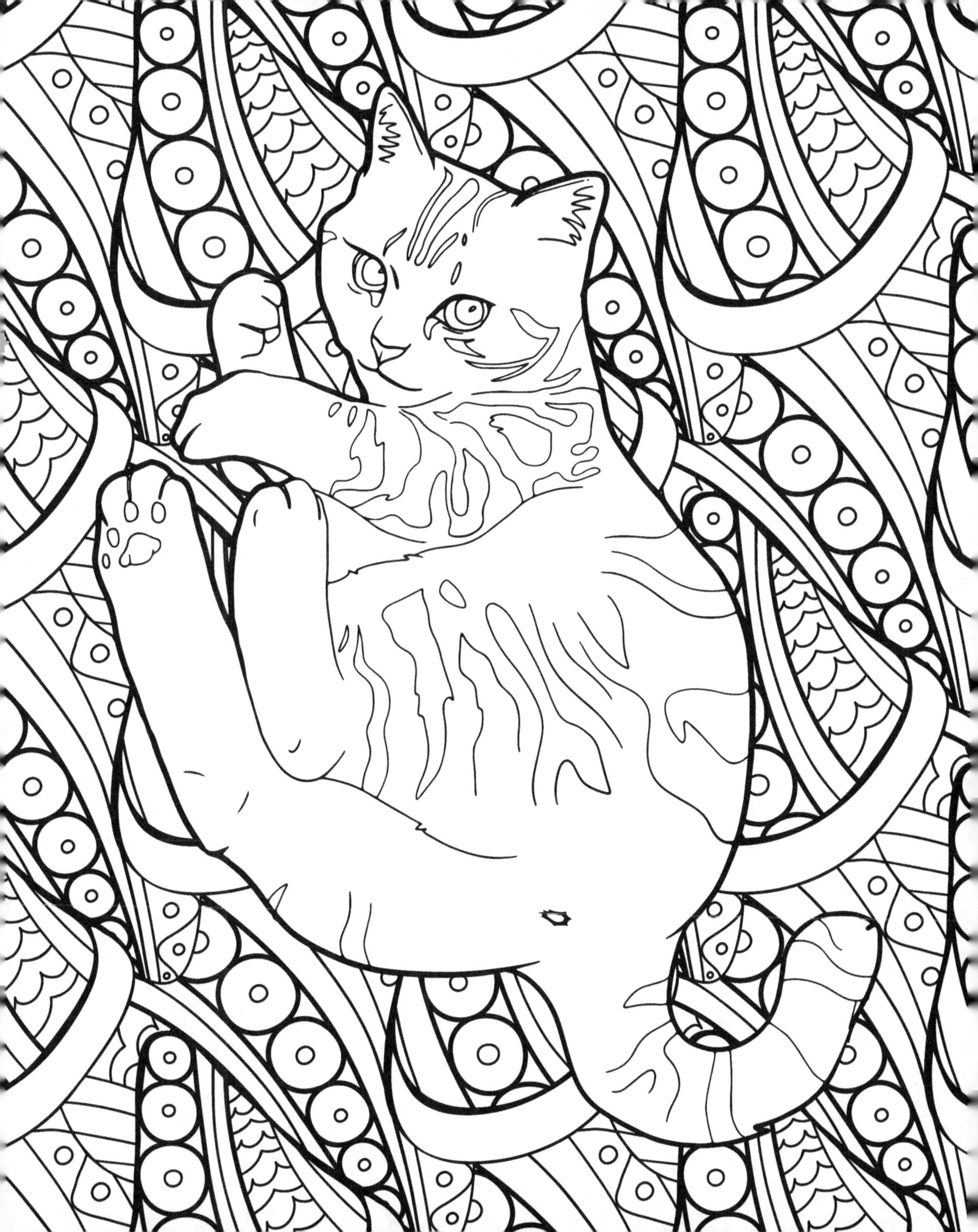

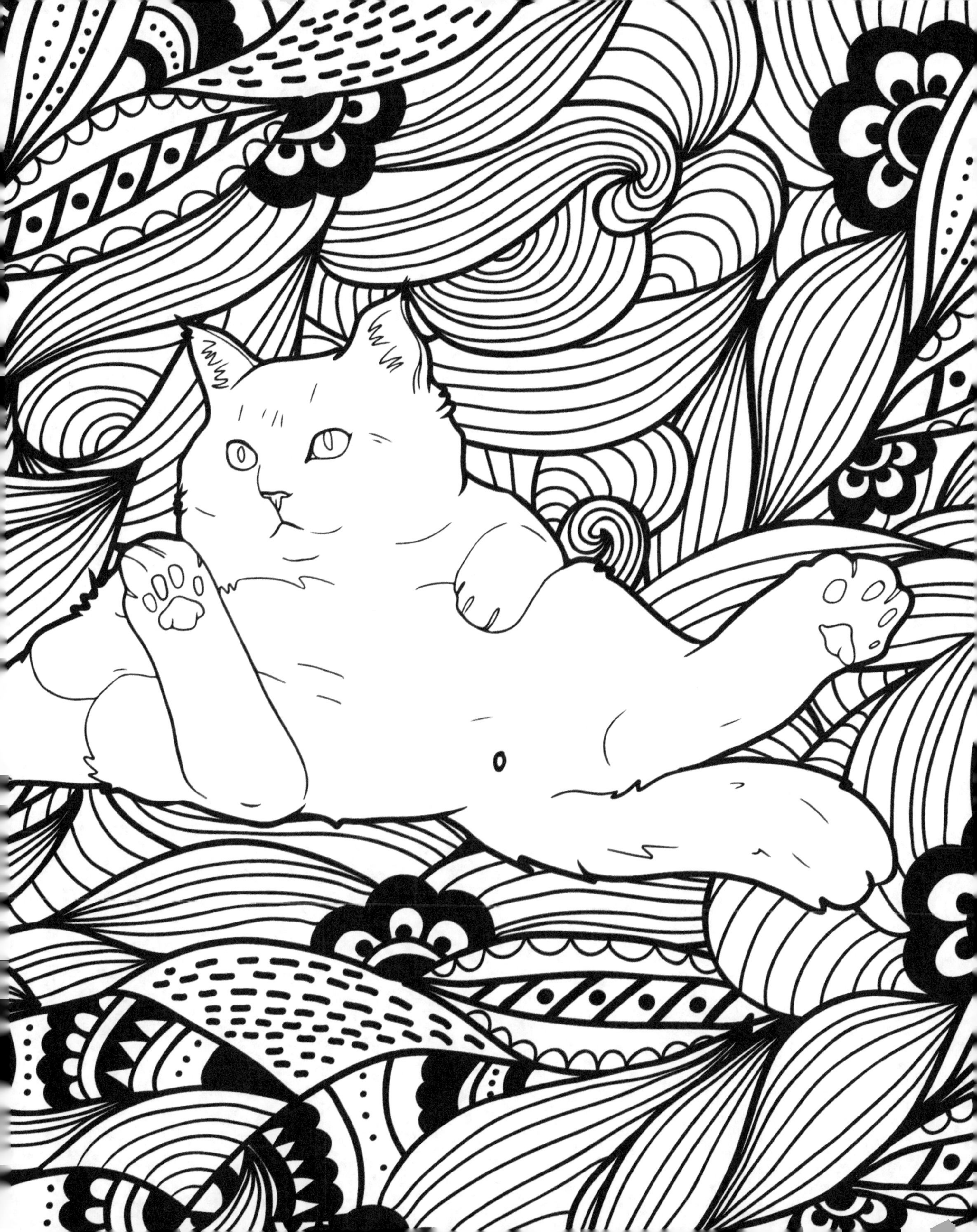

www.ingramcontent.com/pod-product-compliance
Lightning Source LLC
Chambersburg PA
CBHW080523030726
47592CB00012B/3459